We can cook

written by LYNNE PEEBLES

with photographs by TIM CLARK
and JOHN MOYES

Illustrations by JAMES HODGSON

Ladybird Books   Loughborough

Preparation

OVEN TEMPERATURES

Gas	Electricity	
Mark	Fahrenheit (F)	Celsius (C)
2	300°	150°
3	325°	160°
4	350°	180°
5	375°	190°
6	400°	200°
7	425°	220°
8	450°	230°

(Conversions are approximate)

Remember these simple rules when you cook

Always have a grown-up with you when you cook – it's SAFER that way!

Always wash your hands and wear an apron. (And NEVER lick your fingers!)

Always measure carefully.

Always read the recipe right through before you start.

Always leave the kitchen clean and tidy.

Always put your pets out of the kitchen when you are going to cook. They may carry germs which could get into your food.

Measuring

Fats-butter, margarine & lard

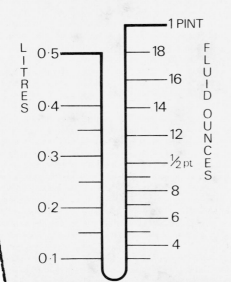

When an average pack (227g or 8 oz) of butter, margarine or lard is divided into eight, each portion may be taken to weigh approximately 25g (1 ounce).

Using scales

Some cooks measure using spoons, but it is more usual to measure using kitchen scales, of which there are many different types.

If you use a tablespoon to measure, one rounded tablespoonful of flour or sugar for example, is approximately equal to 25g (1 ounce).

Note

For the purposes of this book, 1 pint is approximately 500 millilitres (ml), 2 pints one litre, and 1 ounce (oz) 25 grams (g).

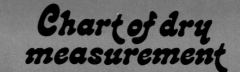

Chart of dry measurement

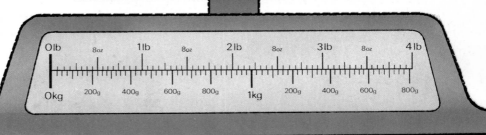

Olb	8oz	1lb	8oz	2lb	8oz	3lb	8oz	4 lb
Okg	200g	400g	600g	800g	1kg	200g	400g	600g	800g

Chart of liquid measurement

LITRES

0·5

0·4

0·3

0·2

0·1

1 PINT

18

16

14

12

½ pt

8

6

4

FLUID OUNCES

Using a spoon

A rounded tablespoon is generally taken to represent 25g or 1 oz. Where a level tablespoon is mentioned in a recipe, use a knife as shown below to level off a heaped tablespoon.

Salads

LETTUCE Tear leaves from stem. Wash in cold water, tear to size, dry in kitchen paper or clean tea towel.

MUSTARD AND CRESS Cut off at base of stem, wash in cold water, drain well.

CUCUMBER Slice very thinly, cut from the centre of the slice to the outside, and open to make a twist.

OR score skin with a fork, all the way round, down the length of the cucumber and slice thinly. The edge will appear crinkly.

SPRING ONIONS Cut off root and trim green top. Slice down towards base several times. Put into iced water to open them up.

CELERY CURLS Wash and scrub celery well in cold water. Cut into 7½ cm (3 inch) lengths. Slice from each end, leaving a small piece uncut in the middle of the length of celery. Place in cold water to curl ends.

CARROTS Take off top and base, scrape or scrub to clean. Using a potato peeler, peel thinly down the length of the carrot. Twist or roll the strip of carrot and hold in place with a cocktail stick. Put into iced water. Before serving, remove cocktail stick.

RADISH ROSES Make cuts in the radish from the top towards the base but do not cut right through. Put into iced water to open.

WATERLILY TOMATOES Holding top and base of the tomato firmly and using a small sharp knife, cut round the middle of the tomato, making V-shaped cuts to the centre. Pull apart carefully.

Winter salad

INGREDIENTS
½ green pepper
½ small white cabbage
50g (2 oz) raisins or sultanas
25g (1 oz) chopped nuts
2 carrots
2 red eating apples
1 stick celery
1 tablespoonful lemon juice
1 small onion
Mayonnaise
Salt and pepper

EQUIPMENT
Chopping board
Small sharp knife
Grater
Serving dish
Salad servers

1 Wash and finely shred cabbage. Remove seeds and slice and chop the green pepper.

2 Peel onion and chop (see page 13).

3 Scrub and grate carrots. Scrub and chop celery.

4 Wash apples, remove core and chop. Mix lemon juice with salt and pepper, and dip the apples in to prevent them discolouring.

5 Place all ingredients in a serving dish. Toss them in mayonnaise and serve.

Serve with: Cheese and onion pasties or Cornish pasties (see page 46).

Fruit & cheese salad

INGREDIENTS
200g (8 oz) cottage cheese
50g (2 oz) peanuts
2 pineapple rings
Teaspoonful chopped chives or parsley
50g (2 oz) black or green grapes
1 banana
Few lettuce leaves or 1 box of mustard and cress
Salt and pepper and lemon juice

EQUIPMENT
Mixing bowl
Small sharp knife
Chopping board
Shallow serving dish

1 Mix together cheese, peanuts, chopped pineapple and parsley or chives.

2 Arrange washed lettuce leaves or mustard and cress around the sides of a serving dish.

3 Pile cheese mixture in the centre. Surround with halved grapes (remember to remove pips) and sliced banana. Sprinkle with lemon juice, salt and pepper, and serve.

Open rolls
Make them look interesting

Instead of making sandwiches, try open rolls; they are as delicious to eat as they are to look at. When shopping, choose long finger rolls or round rolls.

1 Cut rolls in half and spread each cut side with butter.

2 *Toppings:* Choose one or more foods from each column and arrange food attractively on top of rolls:

Sliced ham	Cress
Corned beef	Lettuce
Cheese, sliced or	Cucumber
grated	Sliced tomato
Hard-boiled egg	Tomato wedges
Salmon or tuna	Raisins
mixed with a	Halved grapes
little mayonnaise	Orange slices
	Pineapple

How about
Lettuce and ham with tomato on a cocktail stick?
A slice of orange for a sail?
Lettuce with sliced cheese sail, and grape on top of mast?
Scrambled egg and cress with orange wings?
Salmon and mayonnaise with cucumber wing?

6

Rice salad

INGREDIENTS
100g (4 oz) long grain rice
50g (2 oz) peas
1 small red pepper
1 onion
1 carrot
25g (1 oz) raisins
1 teaspoonful salt
Salt and pepper and lemon juice

EQUIPMENT
Large pan
Chopping board
Small sharp knife
Sieve or colander

1 Put 1 litre (2 pints) of water and 1 teaspoonful of salt in the pan and bring to the boil.

2 Remove seeds from pepper. Chop finely.

3 Peel and chop onion (see page 13). Peel or scrub carrot and cut into small cubes.

4 When water has boiled, add rice, pepper, onion, carrot, and peas and boil steadily without a lid for 10 minutes or until rice is just cooked.

5 Remove from heat. Drain using the sieve or colander and wash well in cold water. Drain thoroughly. Add raisins and mix well.

6 Season with salt and pepper and lemon juice before serving.

Serve with Quiche (see page 49).

Stuffed eggs

INGREDIENTS
4 eggs
1 tablespoonful mustard and cress
Pinch of dry mustard
Salt and pepper
Teaspoonful mayonnaise

EQUIPMENT
Small pan
Chopping board
Teaspoon
Knife and fork
Basin
Serving dish

1 Place eggs in a small pan of cold water, bring to the boil and time for 10 minutes. Plunge eggs into cold water. Leave to cool.

2 Shell the eggs.

3 Cut in half. Using a teaspoon, remove yolk and place it in a small basin. Add cress, mustard, salt and pepper and mayonnaise. Mix well together.

4 Place the egg white cases on a serving dish, place a teaspoonful of the mixture into each egg white case, and arrange in an attractive mound with a fork.

Surround with prepared salad ingredients.

Indian eggs

Follow the method for Stuffed eggs but replace the mustard and cress with 25g (1 oz) of butter and $\frac{1}{4}$ teaspoonful of curry powder.
Mix well together. Pile into egg white cases.

Easy meals

Scrambled egg

INGREDIENTS
2 eggs
25g (1 oz) margarine
1 tablespoonful milk
1 slice bread and a little butter
Salt and pepper

EQUIPMENT
Small pan
Wooden spoon
Small basin
Fork
Tablespoon
Plate

1 Put plate to warm and butter bread.

2 Gently melt margarine in pan on a low heat. Remove from heat.

3 Add 1 tablespoonful milk.

4 Break each egg in turn into the small basin (to make sure it's fresh) and add to the pan.

5 Add a pinch of salt and a shake of pepper.

6 Stir well. Cook the mixture over a low heat stirring all the time with a wooden spoon.

7 Gradually the eggs will thicken. Scrambled eggs should be soft and creamy. Do not overcook or they will become tough and leathery.

Variations

Mix in a little chopped parsley *before* cooking; stir in 25g (1 oz) grated cheese *after* cooking; serve on toast or with fried bread; serve with crispy bacon or fresh tomato.
Eggs should be stored in a cool place, blunt end uppermost.

Welsh rarebit

INGREDIENTS
12½ g (½ oz) butter
100g (4 oz) grated Cheddar cheese
1 tablespoonful milk
Worcestershire sauce
Salt and pepper
2 slices of hot buttered toast

EQUIPMENT
Small pan
Wooden spoon
Knife

1 Turn on the grill.

2 Make two slices of toast and butter them. Put ready on a plate. TURN OFF GRILL.

3 Melt butter in the pan on a low heat.

4 Remove from heat and stir in cheese, milk, Worcestershire sauce, salt and pepper.

5 Return to heat and gently stir with a wooden spoon until all cheese has melted. Do not boil.

6 Spread on toast and serve.

Variations
You can serve with crispy bacon, or put a few thin slices of tomato on top of the rarebit and put it under the grill for a few minutes before serving.

Scotch eggs

INGREDIENTS
(for 4 people)
4 eggs
200g (8 oz) sausage meat
Small cupful brown breadcrumbs
A little milk
A little flour

EQUIPMENT
Rolling pin
Baking sheet
Greaseproof paper or foil
Plates
Small pan
Tablespoon
Fork
Serving dish

1 Put oven on at Gas Mark 5 (electricity 375°F/190°C).

2 Place eggs in small pan of cold water, bring to the boil and time eggs for 10 minutes.

3 While eggs are boiling, divide sausage meat into 4 pieces, and lightly flour a clean table top. Sprinkle a little flour onto the rolling pin and a little onto the sausage meat. Roll out each piece of sausage meat to the size of a saucer.

4 When eggs are cooked, empty away the hot water, fill pan with cold water and leave eggs to cool for a few minutes.

5 Put breadcrumbs on a plate. Pour a little milk onto another plate.

6 Take shells off eggs. Rinse in cold water and place one egg in centre of each piece of sausage meat.

7 Wrap sausage meat around each egg and pinch joins gently together.

8 Using a spoon and fork, dip each Scotch egg first into milk then into breadcrumbs.

9 Reshape if necessary on table top.

10 Wrap each Scotch egg in foil or greaseproof paper, and place on baking sheet.

11 Bake in the oven for 45 minutes and then allow them to cool.

12 Serve cut in half with crisp salad.

Scotch eggs can be served with any of the salads on pages 4 to 7.

Cheese baked potatoes

INGREDIENTS
(8 portions)
4 medium-sized old potatoes
100g (4 oz) grated Cheddar cheese
50g (2 oz) butter or margarine
1 tablespoonful milk
1 sliced tomato
Salt and pepper

EQUIPMENT
Baking sheet
Fork
Teaspoon
Small sharp knife
Grater
Plate
Basin
Flat serving dish
8 paper napkins

1 Put oven on at Gas Mark 6 (electricity 400°F/200°C).

2 Scrub potatoes well in plenty of cold water. Prick each one with a fork 6 times. Put onto baking sheet.

3 Place in oven for approximately 1 hour until cooked. (*To test:* Push the point of knife into the centre of the potato; the knife will slide in and out easily when potato is cooked.)

4 When potatoes are cooked, cut in half lengthways. Scoop out centre with a teaspoon, and put into a basin.

5 Add milk, margarine, salt and pepper and three-quarters of the grated cheese. Mix well.

6 Pile potato mixture back into potato shells. Sprinkle remaining cheese on top.

7 Return potatoes to the oven for 20–30 minutes or until cheese melts and browns.

8 Top each potato with a slice of tomato.

9 Place each potato on a paper napkin and then onto serving dish.

Variations
Chopped parsley or ham may also be added when potato mixture is made.

11

Cheese and potato pie

INGREDIENTS
(*for 4 people*)
Large packet of instant potato (500 ml or 1 pint size)
6 rounded tablespoonfuls (150g or 6 oz) grated Cheddar cheese
1 tomato
25g (1 oz) margarine

EQUIPMENT
Ovenproof serving dish
Mixing bowl
Sharp knife
Table knife
Fork
Pan

1 Put oven on at Gas Mark 4 (electricity 350°F/180°C).

2 Measure 500 ml (1 pint) of water, pour into pan. Place on cooker and bring to boil.

3 Put instant potato in mixing bowl, with margarine. When water boils, carefully pour it onto potato powder, then mix with fork.

4 Add 4 tablespoonfuls of grated cheese to the potato and mix well. Place potato mixture in serving dish and smooth top with knife.

5 Sprinkle on remaining cheese. Place pie in oven for 20 minutes. (If pie is required at once, however, it can be placed under a hot grill until cheese melts and bubbles.)

6 Cut tomato into slices and place on top just before serving. A piece of watercress in each corner also makes this dish look attractive.

Meatballs in oxtail soup

INGREDIENTS

400g (16 oz) minced beef
1 small onion
1 tablespoonful raisins or sultanas
Pinch of salt and pepper
1 medium can of oxtail soup

EQUIPMENT

Ovenproof casserole
Mixing bowl
Sharp knife
Plate
Fork
Tablespoon
Tin opener

1 Put oven on at Gas Mark 4 (electricity 350°F/180°C).

2 Chop onion with a sharp knife (see below).

3 Place chopped onion in mixing bowl, add meat, sultanas or raisins, and salt and pepper. Mix well together using a fork.

4 Shape into 8 balls (using your hands); put them in the bottom of a casserole.

5 Pour the soup over the meatballs.

6 Place lid on casserole. Cook in centre of oven for $1\frac{1}{4}$ hours.

7 Serve with potatoes and a green vegetable such as peas.

Preparing onions

Onions have a strong smell which is released when the onions are chopped and the onion cells are cut. Your eyes may water when you prepare onions. To prevent this, try rinsing onions in cold water after peeling and before chopping. If your eyes *do* water, don't rub them; this will only make them worse.

1 Slice the onion but do not cut right through. Now slice across the other way still not cutting right through.

2 Turn the onion on its side and slice. You will now get small diced pieces.

Meatballs served with Spaghetti

INGREDIENTS
(for 3–4 people)
150g–200g (6 oz–8 oz) spaghetti
25g (1 oz) butter
75g (3 oz) grated cheese or 2 tablespoonfuls Parmesan cheese
1 teaspoonful salt

1 Boil a large pan of water (2 pints/ 1 litre) and add salt.

2 When water is boiling rapidly add spaghetti. Hold it firmly, lower and bend into pan pushing from the end furthest away from the boiling water.

3 Cook without lid for about 10 minutes until just soft. To test, cut through one strand against side of pan; no white centre should be visible.

4 Drain and place in serving dish with butter. Top with meatballs and sprinkle with cheese.

Meatballs served with Rice
A mild but tasty 'curry'

INGREDIENTS
(for 3–4 people)
150g–200g (6 oz–8 oz) long grain rice (Patna)
1 teaspoonful salt
Curry powder

1 To basic meatball mixture add 1 dessertspoonful of curry powder.

2 Boil 1 litre (2 pints) of water and add salt.

3 When boiling add rice and cook without lid for 10 minutes until just soft. To test, with a spoon take out a grain of rice and squash it with your thumbnail. No white centre should be visible.

4 Drain well, and rinse several times in very hot water, drain.

5 Place a border of rice on serving dish and place meatballs in centre.

Can be served with simple side dishes to give variety.
e.g. Pineapple pieces, mixed with chopped apple
Thinly sliced onion and finely chopped tomato in a dressing of lemon juice
Parsley, salt and pepper
Sliced banana
Desiccated coconut

Beefburgers

INGREDIENTS

200g (8 oz) fresh minced beef (will make 4)
Pinch of salt and pepper
1 small onion
A little beaten egg
50g (2 oz) lard or 2 tablespoonfuls cooking oil
A little flour

EQUIPMENT

Frying pan
Fish slice
Mixing bowl
Sharp knife
Fork
Tablespoon
Plate
Serving plate

1 Put minced beef in a mixing bowl with a little salt and pepper.

2 Top, tail and skin onion. Cut into small pieces (see page 13).

3 Add enough egg (about 2 tablespoonfuls) to bind the mixture together. Mix with a fork and divide the mixture into four.

4 On a floured surface, make each one into a round flat shape.

5 Melt the fat in the pan over a low heat. Use a fish slice to add the beef-burgers to the pan. Fry on both sides until cooked right through.

American style

Make up beefburgers following basic recipe, adding one or more of the following:
Teaspoonful chopped parsley
Level teaspoonful made mustard
25g (1 oz) grated cheese

Shape and fry as usual, meanwhile toast the cut side of 4 soft rolls.
Cover with lettuce and sliced tomato and top with cooked beefburgers.
Add sauce or relish to taste and serve immediately.

Substantial enough for a man-sized snack, ideal for a tasty supper, or for picnics or barbecues.

15

Desserts

Separating an egg

1 Break egg onto saucer.

2 Place an egg cup carefully over the yolk. Push down gently.

3 Holding egg cup and saucer, pour off egg white into bowl, leaving egg yolk on saucer.

Note *If egg whites are needed for whisking there must be no egg yolk broken into them. If this happens the egg whites will not whisk up stiffly but will remain soft.*

Chocolate mousse

INGREDIENTS
2 eggs
50g (2 oz) chocolate

EQUIPMENT

Plate
Small pan
Whisk
Small basin
Mixing bowl
Tablespoon
2 small serving dishes

1 Half fill pan with water and allow to boil. Turn off heat.

2 Break chocolate into pieces, and put in small basin. Place basin over hot water, making sure basin does not touch water.

3 Carefully separate eggs. Place whites in mixing bowl and yolks on plate.

4 Whisk whites until they stand in firm peaks.

5 Remove basin from pan. Stir egg yolks into chocolate.

6 Add chocolate mixture to egg whites, and fold in very lightly with tablespoon or knife. If mixed too much the mousse will not set.

7 Pour into dishes. Leave in cool place to set.

Chocolate Mousse when set can be decorated with:

a small amount of grated chocolate; angelica leaves and cherry flowers (a glacé cherry cut into 8 makes the flowers, with leaves cut from thin strips of angelica).

Vanilla icecream

INGREDIENTS

2 eggs
50g (2 oz) icing sugar
¼ teaspoonful vanilla essence
1 packet Bird's Dream Topping
125 ml (¼ pint) milk

EQUIPMENT

Mixing bowl
2 small basins
Whisk
Tablespoon
Teaspoon
Plastic container or ice tray

Set refrigerator to its coldest setting, and choose a container for your icecream that will fit into the ice-making compartment.

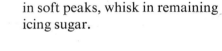

1 Empty Dream Topping into a mixing bowl and whisk with 125 ml (¼ pint) milk until smooth.

2 Separate eggs (see page 17). Put yolks in one small basin, and put whites in the other small basin.

3 Add half the icing sugar to the egg yolks with ¼ teaspoonful vanilla essence and mix well.

4 Whisk egg whites until standing in soft peaks, whisk in remaining icing sugar.

5 Add yolk mixture, and egg whites, to the Dream Topping and whisk well. Pour into freezing container.

6 Freeze for at least two hours until firm.

Flavoured icecream

Instead of using vanilla essence, you could try:

Rum and raisin (¼ teaspoonful rum essence, 25g–50g (1 oz–2 oz) raisins).

Chocolate (make vanilla icecream first, then add grated or chopped chocolate together with a little cocoa or drinking chocolate if desired).

Strawberry or raspberry (in summer 100g (4 oz) of fresh fruit can be whisked into the Dream Topping).

When not available, substitute two tablespoonfuls of milk shake syrup.

Peach melba

INGREDIENTS
(for 4–6 people)

1 medium can peach halves
A little strawberry syrup
A few split almonds
4–6 cherries
4–6 scoops icecream
8–12 icecream wafers

EQUIPMENT

4–6 serving dishes
Tin opener
Tablespoon

1 Place half a peach in each dish, cut side uppermost. Top each with a scoop of icecream.
2 Pour on a little syrup. Use split almonds to make leaves, place cherry in centre to make flower.
3 Add wafers.
4 Serve immediately.

Chocolate sauce

INGREDIENTS
75g (3 oz) brown sugar
25g (1 oz) butter
25g (1 oz) cocoa powder
2 tablespoonfuls milk
½ teaspoonful vanilla essence

EQUIPMENT

Small pan
Wooden spoon

1 Place all ingredients in a small pan. Stir over a gentle heat until butter is melted, and the sauce is smooth.
2 Bring to boil and boil stirring well for 3 minutes.
3 Serve hot, poured over icecream.

Butterscotch sauce

INGREDIENTS
25g (1 oz) butter
25g (1 oz) brown sugar
1 tablespoonful golden syrup

EQUIPMENT

Small pan
Wooden spoon

1 Melt butter, sugar and syrup together in a small pan over a low heat.
2 Bring to boil, boil for 1 minute.
3 Before serving, cool slightly and pour over icecream.

Melba sauce

INGREDIENTS
100g (4 oz) strawberry jam
2 tablespoonfuls black currant cordial ('Ribena')
1 teaspoonful cornflour
4 tablespoonfuls water

EQUIPMENT

Wooden spoon
Small pan

1 Blend cornflour with water in a small pan, add other ingredients, and mix well.
2 Heat steadily, bring to the boil, boil for 1 minute.
3 Cool and serve, poured over icecream.

Banana snow

INGREDIENTS
3 bananas
2 egg whites
25g (1 oz) sugar
A little lemon juice
A few drops of food colouring
A little desiccated coconut

EQUIPMENT
Whisk
Mixing bowl
Small basin
Fork
Serving dish (or dishes)

1 Peel the bananas, place in a small basin and mash lightly with a fork, adding a little lemon juice.

2 Place egg whites in mixing bowl, whisk until standing in stiff peaks.

3 Add banana and sugar to egg white and continue whisking until mixture becomes quite stiff.

4 Add a few drops of food colouring, mix well and pour into serving dish or dishes.

5 Put a little desiccated coconut on a plate and pop underneath the grill until brown. Decorate with the toasted coconut.

Note   Any fresh fruit when peeled will discolour in the air. Acid in the form of lemon juice will help to prevent this.

Banana custard

Follow the basic recipe for making custard but increase the amount of custard powder and sugar to 2 rounded tablespoonfuls.

After cooking, add 3 peeled and sliced bananas and pour into a serving dish.

This dish may be served hot or cold. If served cold, decorate with cherries before serving.

Basic custard

INGREDIENTS
500 ml (1 pint) milk
1 rounded and 1 level tablespoonful custard powder
1 rounded and 1 level tablespoonful sugar

EQUIPMENT
Pan
Wooden spoon
Tablespoon

1 Put custard powder and sugar in pan, add a little of the milk and mix to a smooth cream with a wooden spoon, gradually add the rest of the milk.

2 Place on top of the cooker, and heat gently, stirring all the time until custard mixture begins to thicken, then allow to boil for 1 minute, stirring all the time.

3 Remove from heat.

Peach and coconut delight

INGREDIENTS

500 ml (1 pint) custard sauce
Small tin of peaches
1 dessertspoonful powdered gelatine
50g (2 oz) desiccated coconut
Few glacé cherries

EQUIPMENT

Small pan	*Basin*
Can opener	*Knife*
Dessertspoon	
500 ml (1 pint) mould	
Serving plate	

1 Make the custard following the basic recipe.

2 Drain peaches, placing the juice in a small basin.

3 Add the gelatine to the fruit juice, place basin over a pan of hot water and stir until dissolved.

4 Add to hot custard and stir well.

5 Slice the peaches and add to the custard.

6 Pour into a wet mould.

7 Leave in a cool place to set.

8 Toast the coconut as for Banana snow (page 20).

9 Turn mould out into a dish. Arrange a border of coconut around the base, decorate with cherries and any remaining fruit.

Variations

Any type of fruit can be used for this dessert to give a variety of flavour and colour.

Strawberry flummery

INGREDIENTS
1 strawberry jelly
2 eggs
50g (2 oz) caster
sugar

EQUIPMENT
Wooden spoon
Small pan
Mixing bowl
Whisk
Serving dishes
Tablespoon

1 Follow stages 1 and 2 for fresh fruit in jelly (below).

2 Separate yolks from whites of eggs (see page 17.)

3 Whisk yolks with 25g (1 oz) of sugar and 2 tablespoonfuls of water, until thick and creamy.

4 Gradually whisk the cold jelly into the yolk mixture. Leave in a cold place until just beginning to set.

5 Wash and dry whisk. Whisk the egg whites until very stiff. Whisk in remaining 25g (1 oz) of sugar.

6 Whisk into the almost setting jelly.

7 Pour into serving dishes and leave in a cold place to set.

Fresh fruit in jelly

INGREDIENTS
1 jelly
1 apple
1 orange
50g (2 oz) grapes
1 banana

EQUIPMENT
Small pan
Chopping board
Small sharp knife
Wooden spoon
Measuring jug
4 individual dishes
or 500 ml (1 pint) mould

1 Place jelly in a small pan, add 125 ml ($\frac{1}{4}$ pint) water, heat gently, stirring until jelly has dissolved.

2 Pour into measuring jug and make up to 375 ml ($\frac{3}{4}$ pint) with cold water. Put in a cold place to begin setting.

3 Prepare fruit. Grapes: Wash and cut in half. Take out pips. Orange: Remove top and bottom cutting through to flesh. Cut off peel and pith, pull orange apart, taking segments out carefully. Apple: Peel, cut into quarters, remove core and roughly chop. Banana: Peel and slice.

4 Stir fruit into jelly mixture, pour into mould or serving dishes. Leave in cold place to set.

Quick note

To help the jelly to set quickly, at stage 2, make up to 375 ml ($\frac{3}{4}$ pint) with icecubes instead of cold water.

Golden crunchies

INGREDIENTS

1 rounded tablespoonful sugar (25g or 1 oz)
2 cups Kellogg's Rice Krispies or Cornflakes (75g or 3 oz)
25g (1 oz) margarine
2 rounded tablespoonfuls golden syrup
20 paper cake cases

EQUIPMENT

Mixing bowl
Tablespoon
Wooden spoon
Small pan
Knife

1 Spread cake cases out on a work top.

2 Put Rice Krispies into mixing bowl. Place margarine, sugar and golden syrup in the pan, place on top of the cooker and heat *very gently*, stirring with wooden spoon until the margarine, sugar and golden syrup have melted together. Boil for 1 minute. Remove from heat.

3 Pour melted mixture into Rice Krispies, and stir gently until they are all coated. When pan is empty, fill it with cold water.

4 Using a tablespoon and the knife put mixture into each cake case, then leave them in a cool place to set.

5 Clear away and wash up. Wash pan last of all.

Small cakes

Coconut pyramids

INGREDIENTS
75g (3 oz) desiccated coconut
75g (3 oz) caster sugar
1 egg white
2 glacé cherries (cut into quarters)

EQUIPMENT
Mixing bowl
Whisk
Wooden spoon
Teaspoon
Egg cup
Baking sheet (nonstick or greased)

1 Put oven on at Gas Mark 4 (electricity 350°F/180°C).

2 Place the egg white in a mixing bowl. Whisk until white and fluffy.

3 Add sugar and coconut and mix well.

4 Dip egg cup in water and then fill with mixture.

5 Shake out gently onto baking sheet. Repeat with rest of mixture.

6 Top each pyramid with a piece of glacé cherry.

7 Bake for 15–20 minutes until the cakes are a light golden brown.

Cherry tops

INGREDIENTS

2 rounded tablespoonfuls sugar (50g or 2 oz)
50g (2 oz) margarine
1 egg
2 rounded tablespoonfuls self-raising flour (50g or 2 oz)
5 cherries

EQUIPMENT

10 paper cake cases
Mixing bowl
Wooden spoon
Tablespoon
Small basin
Bun tins
Table knife
2 teaspoons
Serving plate
Sieve

1 Put oven on at Gas Mark 5 (electricity 375°F/190°C).

2 Cut the cherries in half.

3 Put margarine and sugar in mixing bowl, add sifted flour.

4 Crack the egg into the small basin (just to make sure it is fresh), then add to the things in the mixing bowl.

5 Mix everything together with a wooden spoon, until smooth and creamy.

6 Put a teaspoonful of mixture into each cake case.

7 Place the bun tray carefully in the oven, and bake the cakes for 15 minutes. When the cakes are cooked, they will be golden brown and firm.

8 Remove cases from bun tray, top each cake with half of a cherry, and leave to cool.

Flapjacks

INGREDIENTS

1 full tablespoonful golden syrup
(approx. 75g or 3 oz)
75g (3 oz) sugar
75g (3 oz) margarine
150g (6 oz) rolled oats
Pinch of salt
A little lard for greasing

EQUIPMENT

18 cm (7 in) cake tin
Small pan
Tablespoon
Teaspoon
Wooden spoon
Mixing bowl
18 cm (7 in) circle greaseproof
paper

1 Put oven on at Gas Mark 3
   (electricity 325°F/160°C).

2 Grease inside of tin and line with
   greaseproof paper (see page 31).

3 Place golden syrup, margarine
   and sugar in pan. Put oats and
   pinch of salt in mixing bowl.

4 Using a wooden spoon, stir
   ingredients in the pan over a low
   heat until just melted.

5 Pour into oats and mix well.

6 Put mixture in cake tin and press
   down, levelling off top as shown
   below.

7 Place in the oven for 20 minutes
   until just firm in the centre.

8 Remove from the oven.

9 Mark into portions while still hot.

10 Turn out of tin when cool.

Cherry and almond fingers

INGREDIENTS

Base:
75g (3 oz) plain flour
25g (1 oz) sugar
50g (2 oz) margarine

Middle:
75g (3 oz) glacé cherries
25g (1 oz) sultanas

Top:
50g (2 oz) butter
50g (2 oz) sugar
50g (2 oz) ground almonds
1 egg

EQUIPMENT

20 cm (8 in) square cake tin
Mixing bowl
Wooden spoon
Knife
Plate
Greaseproof paper
Serving dish

1 Put oven on at Gas Mark 5 (electricity 375°F/190°C).

2 Cut greaseproof paper to fit base of tin.

3 Place ingredients for base in mixing bowl, rub fat into flour and sugar with fingertips. Gather dough together and press down well into base of tin.

4 Cut cherries into quarters and sprinkle on top of base with sultanas.

5 Place topping ingredients in mixing bowl and mix together with a wooden spoon until smooth and creamy.

6 Spread on top of ingredients in the tin.

7 Bake for 40 minutes in the centre of the oven until firm to touch in centre.

8 Take out of oven and leave to cool in tin. Cut up into sixteen fingers.

Butterfly cakes

All-in-one method

INGREDIENTS

100g (4 oz) caster sugar
100g (4 oz) soft margarine
100g (4 oz) self-raising flour
2 level teaspoonfuls baking powder
2 eggs

EQUIPMENT

Mixing bowl
Sieve
Wooden spoon
Teaspoon
Knife
20 paper cake cases
Baking tray

1 Put oven on at Gas Mark 5 (electricity 375°F/190°C).

2 Place the sugar, margarine and eggs in the mixing bowl.

3 Sift the flour and baking powder over the other ingredients.

4 Beat all these together for 2–3 minutes with a wooden spoon.

5 Spoon the mixture into the 20 paper cake cases and stand them on a baking tray.

6 Place in the oven for 15 minutes or until golden brown. Allow to cool before decorating.

Butter icing

INGREDIENTS

250g (10 oz) icing sugar
125g (5 oz) butter

EQUIPMENT

Teaspoon
Small mixing bowl
Wooden spoon
Sieve
Sharp pointed knife

1 Sieve the icing sugar into the bowl.

2 Add the butter and mix them together with the wooden spoon until soft and creamy.

3 Cover mixture with a clean damp cloth until you are ready to use it.

4 Using a sharp knife, carefully cut a circle out of the top of each cake.

5 Cut this circle of cake in half to make 2 butterfly wings.

6 Spoon a little of the butter icing onto the top of each cake and put the two 'wings' on top of the icing.

Variations & flavourings

To the basic cake mixture, *one* of the following can be added:
Orange – add grated rind of one orange: Chocolate or coffee – add 1 dessertspoonful of cocoa or coffee dissolved in 1 tablespoonful of water: Coffee and Walnut – as for coffee with 50g (2 oz) chopped walnuts.

28

Gingerbread men

INGREDIENTS

100g (4 oz) plain flour
½ level teaspoonful bicarbonate of soda
25g (1 oz) brown sugar
50g (2 oz) margarine
75g (3 oz) golden syrup
1 level teaspoonful ground ginger
Currants for decoration
50g (2 oz) plain flour for shaping

EQUIPMENT

Baking sheet
Mixing bowl
Wooden spoon
Tablespoon
Sieve
Teaspoon

1 Put oven on at Gas Mark 5 (electricity 375°F/190°C).

2 Cream margarine and sugar together, add the golden syrup and ground ginger and mix well.

3 Sift in flour and the bicarbonate of soda.

4 Mix well together.

5 Turn onto a well floured board and work some of the flour into the surface of the dough.

6 Divide dough into 12 pieces and cut each piece into 3. Shape a small round head, a sausage shape for the arms, and a longer sausage shape for the legs. Press flat on a baking tray and bend legs and arms. Add currants for eyes and buttons.

7 Bake for 10–12 minutes, until golden brown and firm at the edges. (The centre will remain soft until they are cold).

You can make endless different men, with a bit of imagination, or you can roll and cut out the dough with animal cutters.

Large cakes

Creaming method

INGREDIENTS
100g (4 oz) caster sugar
100g (4 oz) margarine
100g (4 oz) self-raising flour
2 eggs

EQUIPMENT
Mixing bowl
Wooden spoon
Small basin
Fork
Sieve
Tablespoon

1 Put oven on at Gas Mark 4 (electricity 350°F/180°C).

2 Place margarine in the bowl and soften with a wooden spoon.

3 Add the sugar and beat well together with the wooden spoon until pale and creamy.

4 Break the eggs into the small basin and beat with a fork. Gradually add beaten egg to the creamed mixture, a tablespoonful at a time, beating well before each addition. If too much egg is added, the mixture may begin to curdle. To correct this, either stand the bowl in hot water and beat the mixture well or add one tablespoonful of sieved flour.

5 When all the egg has been added, gently fold in sifted flour using a metal spoon.

6 Grease and line with greaseproof paper whichever tin you are using (see right) and place the mixture in the tin.

7 Put in the oven and bake until firm and golden brown. Cooking time will depend on the shape and size of tin. 18 cm (7 in) tin, 20 mins. Swiss Roll tins 26 cm × 18 cm (11 in × 7 in), 15–20 mins. Loaf tins 400g (1 lb), 30–40 mins.

Traditional Victoria sandwich

INGREDIENTS
Basic mixture described page 30
2 tablespoonfuls plum jam

EQUIPMENT
2 × 18 cm (7 in) sandwich tins
Wire cake rack

1 Make the creamed mixture described on page 30 and divide it between the two greased and lined sandwich tins. (See preparation of tins).

2 When cooked, turn the two cakes out onto a wire rack and leave them to cool. Cover with a clean damp tea towel.

3 Spread two tablespoonfuls of plum jam on one of the cakes and put the other cake on top to form a sandwich.

4 Sprinkle caster sugar on the top and serve.

Variations

To the basic creamed mixture you can add any one of the following or any of the flavourings suggested for the all-in-one method cakes on page 28. Lemon cake – grated rind of one lemon.   Almond cake – add 50g (2 oz) almonds and a few drops of ground almond essence.

Preparation of tins

CAKE TINS – Brush base and sides with vegetable oil or lard. Cut circle of greaseproof paper to fit base.

LOAF TINS, SWISS ROLL TINS. Brush base and sides with vegetable oil or lard. Stand tin in centre of a piece of greaseproof paper which is bigger than the base by as many cm (in) as the sides are deep. Mark base corners and cut to corners. Place in tin. Fold corners to lie flat.

Glacé icing

This is a water icing and the exact measurement of water and icing sugar is very important. This icing is not used for the centre of a cake but for the top and sides.

INGREDIENTS
150g (6 oz)
icing sugar
5–6 × 5 ml
teaspoonfuls
cold water

EQUIPMENT
Basin
Wooden spoon
5 ml teaspoon
Sieve
Table knife

1 Sieve the icing sugar into a basin and add the water.

2 Mix well with a wooden spoon until the mixture will fall off the spoon and find its own level in the bowl. If you need more water, add it carefully drop by drop.

3 Spread the icing over the top of the sandwich cake and, if you wish, also round the sides.

Chocolate gâteau

INGREDIENTS

150g (6 oz) caster sugar
150g (6 oz) margarine
150g (6 oz) self-raising flour
3 eggs (size 2–3)
1 tablespoonful cocoa dissolved in
1 tablespoonful hot water

EQUIPMENT

as for basic mixture page 30
2 × 18 cm (7 in) or 20 cm (8 in)
sandwich tins

1 Put oven on at Gas Mark 4 (electricity 350°F/180°C).

2 Follow the method for either the all-in-one (page 28) or the creamed mixture (page 30).

3 Add the cocoa and mix well.

4 Share the mixture between the two tins and put in the oven.

5 Bake for 25 – 30 minutes.

6 Turn out onto a wire rack and allow to cool.

Decoration

INGREDIENTS

300g (12 oz) icing sugar
150g (6 oz) butter
1 tablespoonful cocoa dissolved in
1 tablespoonful hot water
100g–150g (4 oz–6 oz) chocolate
vermicelli (sugar strands),
chocolate buttons or chocolate flake

EQUIPMENT

Basin
Wooden spoon
Knife
Icing bag
Number 8 or number 14 icing nozzle
Greaseproof paper
Plate

1 Sift icing sugar into a basin and add butter. Cream them both together. Add the liquid cocoa and mix well.

2 Sandwich the two cakes together with a small amount of the butter icing.

3 Spread some of the icing around the sides.

4 Place the vermicelli onto greaseproof paper and using both hands, one on top and one on the base, turn the cake around so that the sides become covered in the sugar strands.

5 Place on a serving plate and sprinkle the top of the cake with icing sugar.

6 Put the remaining icing in an icing bag fitted with a number 8 or 14 nozzle.

7 Pipe a border round the cake top, then take the icing across from side to side finishing with a swirl in the middle. Add chocolate buttons or chocolate flake for decoration.

Swiss roll

Whisked cakes or true sponge cakes contain no fat and do not store or keep very well.

INGREDIENTS
62½g (2½ oz) sugar
50g (2 oz) plain flour
2 eggs (size 2–3)

for finishing the Swiss roll:
12½g (½ oz) caster sugar
2–3 tablespoonfuls jam

EQUIPMENT

Mixing bowl
Rotary whisk
Tablespoon
Sieve
Shallow baking tin or Swiss roll tin
26 cm × 18 cm (11 in × 7 in)
Damp clean tea towel
Sheet greaseproof paper
Sharp knife

1 Grease and line the tin first because this mixture should not wait.

2 Put oven on at Gas Mark 6 (electricity 400°F/200°C).

To roll the cake

1 While the Swiss roll is baking, place a damp teatowel on the work surface and on top of this place a sheet of greaseproof paper. Sprinkle this with caster sugar.

2 Soften jam in a basin with a knife.

3 When Swiss roll is cooked, turn out immediately onto the paper. Remove greaseproof lining from the cake.

4 Trim off all edges of the cake with a sharp knife, cutting straight down.

5 Spread jam over surface to within 1cm (¼ in) of each edge and make a cut almost through the cake about 2.5 cm (1 in) from one of the short edges.

3 Place eggs and sugar in a mixing bowl and whisk steadily for 8–10 minutes. The mixture will lighten in colour and should hold a trail for 10 seconds. (On a cold day the sugar can be warmed to speed up the whisking.)

4 Sift the flour and gently but quickly, using a figure-of-eight movement, fold in the flour with a metal spoon. This stage should take about 30 seconds.

5 Pour immediately into the prepared baking tin.

6 Place in the oven and bake for 8–10 minutes.

6 Fold over along this line and lifting the cake with greaseproof paper, roll to the other end.

7 Hold in place for one minute with the finishing edge on the bottom.

Mandarin and grape gâteau

This is a more expensive recipe and would be suitable for special visitors.

INGREDIENTS

Basic whisked mixture used for Swiss roll page 33

for filling and decoration:
2–3 tablespoonfuls apricot jam
100g (4 oz) desiccated coconut
1 tin mandarin oranges
50g (2 oz) black grapes

125ml (¼ pint) fresh double or whipping cream or butter icing *made from:*
125g (5 oz) icing sugar
50g (2 oz) butter
1 tablespoonful orange fruit syrup

EQUIPMENT

As for basic mixture
1 × 400g (1 lb) loaf tin
Table knife

1 Put oven on at Gas Mark 6 (electricity 400°F/200°C).

2 Grease and line your loaf tin (see page 31).

3 Prepare the mixture as for Swiss roll on page 33, pour into tin and bake in the oven for 10–12 minutes.

4 Meanwhile, open the can of oranges, drain off the juice and wash and halve the grapes.

5 Whip the fresh cream until stiff enough to stand in peaks.
or Make up the butter icing (page 28).

6 Place the coconut on a shallow ovenproof dish, and grill. Turn frequently until evenly brown.

7 When the cake is cool, slice it into three layers lengthways. Spread thin layer of cream and apricot jam between each layer of cake and reassemble it. Now spread apricot jam round the sides of the cake.

8 Carefully dip the sides in the toasted coconut and put the cake onto a serving plate.

9 Put the cream into an icing bag and pipe attractively over the top of the cake using a number 8 or 14 nozzle.

10 Arrange mandarin and grapes in a pattern along the top of the cake.
Any left-over fruit can be arranged at the base of the cake.

Fruit cake

INGREDIENTS

100g (4 oz) caster sugar
100g (4 oz) soft margarine
200g (8 oz) self-raising flour
2 eggs (size 2–3)
100g (4 oz) mixed dried fruit
25g (1 oz) glacé cherries
1 level teaspoonful mixed spice
Pinch of salt, milk to mix

EQUIPMENT

Mixing bowl
Sieve
Wooden spoon
Fork
Teaspoon
Small basin
18 cm (7 in) cake tin
or 400g (1 lb) loaf tin

1 Put oven on at Gas Mark 4 (electricity 350°F/180°C).

2 Sift flour, salt and spice into the bowl and add the sugar.

3 Coat the margarine with flour and cut up into small pieces. Rub in until the mixture looks like large breadcrumbs, then add the fruit.

4 Break the eggs into the basin and beat them using a fork. Add this to the cake mixture with enough milk to make a mixture which falls from the spoon in lumps.

5 Put into the greased and lined cake or loaf tin (see page 31) and place in the oven.

6 Bake for about 1 hour. (Test the cake by sticking a skewer into the centre to see if it is cooked. The skewer should come out clean.)

7 When cooked allow cake to ⸱ slightly befor⸱ wire rack. Remove p⸱.

I⸱ ⸱op oj cake appears to be browning too quickly reduce heat to Gas Mark 3 (electricity 325°F/160°C).

Puddings

Pancakes

The recipe for batter can be used to make Yorkshire pudding.

INGREDIENTS

100g (4 oz) plain flour
Pinch of salt
1 egg + milk to make up to 250 ml
(½ pint)
Lard for frying

EQUIPMENT

Small frying pan
Serving plate
Whisk
Sieve
Palette knife

1 Sift flour and salt into a bowl. Make a well in the centre of the flour.

2 Beat egg and milk together.

3 Gradually add beaten egg and a little milk to flour mixture and stir well.

4 Work in rest of liquid and mix to a smooth batter. (If any lumps occur, whisk well.) Chill before using.

5 Melt a little lard in a heavy frying pan. Tilt so that the fat covers base, empty away any excess.

BE VERY CAREFUL WITH HOT FAT

6 Pour a little batter mixture into the pan and tilt so that the mixture covers the base. More mixture can be added if needed but pancakes should not be too thick. Cook for 2–3 minutes until set. Free edges with palette knife and shake pan gently to free centre. Turn the pancake over.

7 Cook for a further 2–3 minutes. Turn onto warm plate and serve hot with fresh lemon or orange juice.

Apple and raisin pancakes

INGREDIENTS

Basic pancake mixture
200g (4 oz) cooking apples
50g (2 oz) granulated sugar
25g (1 oz) raisins
1 tablespoonful water

EQUIPMENT

Small pan
Vegetable peeler
Sharp knife

1 Peel, core and slice the apples. Place in small pan with the other ingredients.

2 Heat gently until apples are soft. Spread on pancakes and roll up.

3 Serve with custard or cream.

   For jam, lemon curd, or honey pancakes, spread pancakes with filling, roll up and serve.

Bread and butter pudding

INGREDIENTS

4 slices white bread
25g (1 oz) butter
50g (2 oz) mixed dried fruit
25g (1 oz) caster sugar
1 egg
250 ml ($\frac{1}{2}$ pint) milk

EQUIPMENT

500 ml (1 pint) ovenproof dish
Knife and fork
Measuring jug

1 Put oven on at Gas Mark 4 (electricity 350°F/180°C).

2 Carefully cut off crusts from bread and spread the four slices with butter. Grease the dish. Place crusts in the bottom.

3 Cut each slice of bread into four, either squares or triangles.

4 Arrange pieces of bread over the crusts and around the sides of the dish and sprinkle some of the fruit and sugar over the bread.

5 Put in another layer of bread, the rest of the fruit and some of the sugar.

6 Cover this with the rest of the bread with the buttered side up. Sprinkle with the rest of the sugar.

7 Beat the egg well into the milk and gently pour over the pudding. Let this stand for 10 minutes so that the bread will soak up the milk.

8 Put into oven and bake for 30–45 minutes until set and the top is crisp and golden.

9 Serve immediately.

Lemon surprise pudding

INGREDIENTS
1 packet lemon pie filling
2 eggs
1 small tin pineapple pieces
2 rounded tablespoonfuls sugar
(50g or 2 oz)

EQUIPMENT

Small pan
Wooden spoon
Whisk
Measuring jug
Metal spoon
2 ovenproof dishes
Mixing bowl
Tin opener

1 Put oven on at Gas Mark 4
   (electricity 350°F/180°C).

2 Open tin of pineapple, place
   juice in a measuring jug and add
   water to make up to 250 ml
   ($\frac{1}{2}$ pint).

3 Separate eggs (see page 17). Place
   yolks and lemon pie filling in
   pan; place whites in mixing bowl.

4 Add the 250 ml ($\frac{1}{2}$ pint) mixed
   juice and water to the egg yolks.

5 Place pan on top of cooker and
   heat gently, stirring all the time,
   until the lemon mixture comes to
   the boil and thickens.

6 Add pineapple pieces to lemon
   sauce and stir well. Pour into the
   ovenproof dishes.

7 Whisk egg whites until they stand
   in soft peaks; add the sugar and
   fold in with metal spoon.

8 Spoon mixture on top of lemon
   sauce in dishes, working from the
   sides to the centre. Bring mixture
   up into peaks using the back of a
   metal spoon.

9 Place dishes in the centre of the
   oven for 15 minutes until the
   peaks are golden brown. This
   pudding can be served hot or cold.

Variation

If liked, a biscuit base may be
made to change the pudding
into a simple flan.

1 Crush 8 digestive biscuits
   in a mixing bowl, using the
   end of a rolling pin.

2 Melt 50g (2 oz) butter
   gently in a small pan, add
   to crushed biscuits and mix
   well. Place biscuit mixture
   in base of serving dish and
   press down well. Place
   lemon mixture and egg
   white mixture on top of
   biscuit base. Serve cold.

Eve's pudding

INGREDIENTS

Base: 1 large cooking apple
25g (1 oz) demerara sugar
1 tablespoonful water

Topping: 50g (2 oz) caster sugar
50g (2 oz) margarine
1 egg (size 2–3)
50g (2 oz) self-raising flour

EQUIPMENT

Small sharp knife
Vegetable peeler
Wooden spoon
Mixing bowl
Ovenproof dish
Chopping board
Metal spoon
Small pan

1 Put oven on at Gas Mark 4 (electricity 350°F/180°C).

2 Peel, core and slice apple.

3 Place apple in small pan with water and brown sugar. Heat gently until apple is soft.

4 Grease the ovenproof dish and spread apple mixture over base.

5 Mix the margarine and caster sugar together in the mixing bowl. Beat with the wooden spoon until light and fluffy.

6 Beat the egg and add a little at a time with a little of the flour. Add the rest of the flour and fold it in gently.

7 Spread the mixture over the top of the apple.

8 Bake in the oven for 35 minutes or until well risen and golden brown.

Rhubarb crumble

INGREDIENTS

Topping: 150g (6 oz) plain flour
75g (3 oz) margarine
75g (3 oz) sugar

Base: 400g (16 oz) rhubarb
75g (3 oz) sugar

EQUIPMENT

Ovenproof dish
Mixing bowl
Sieve
Fork
Knife

1 Put oven on at Gas Mark 5 (electricity 375°F/190°C).

2 Sift flour into mixing bowl, add sugar and margarine. Rub margarine into flour and sugar until there are no large lumps of fat and the mixture looks like fine breadcrumbs.

3 Chop rhubarb and place in dish. Sweeten with sugar.

4 Sprinkle on crumble topping and press down well with a fork. Run fork prongs gently over the top to give a crumbly look.

5 Bake in the centre of the oven for 35 minutes, until just brown.

6 Serve with cream or custard.

Variations

You may use either fresh or tinned fruit to vary this recipe. If you use tinned fruit, drain off the juice to serve with the crumble along with cream or custard.
See recipe on page 20 for custard.

Raspberry cap pudding

INGREDIENTS
2 dessertspoonfuls raspberry jam
50g (2 oz) margarine
50g (2 oz) caster sugar
50g (2 oz) self-raising flour
1 egg (size 2–3)
2 dessertspoonfuls warm water

EQUIPMENT
Dessertspoon
Wooden spoon
Mixing bowl
500 ml (1 pint) ovenproof basin
Serving plate

1 Put oven on at Gas Mark 4 (electricity 350°F/180°C).

2 Grease the ovenproof basin.

3 Spoon 2 dessertspoonfuls of raspberry jam into the bottom of the basin.

4 To make the sponge mixture, follow the creaming method as described on page 30, adding the water with the flour.

5 Put the sponge mixture into the basin on top of the jam so that it fills ¾ of the bowl.

6 Put in centre of the oven for 35–45 minutes until it is well risen and golden.
(To test if cooked, stick a skewer into the middle. It should come out clean.)

7 Allow to cool slightly so that the pudding shrinks away from the sides of the basin.

8 Place the serving plate on top of the basin and with a cloth, turn the pudding over and out onto the plate.

9 Serve hot with custard (see page 20).

Pastry dishes

Shortcrust pastry

INGREDIENTS

200g (8 oz) plain flour
50g (2 oz) lard
50g (2 oz) margarine
Pinch of salt
2½ tablespoonfuls cold water

EQUIPMENT

Sieve
Mixing bowl
Table knife
Tablespoon

When making pastry, your hands, the ingredients, and your equipment must all be kept as cool as possible. Start by washing your hands in cold water.

1 Sift flour and salt into mixing bowl. Add margarine and lard and coat these pieces of fat in flour. Cut them up into small pieces with a knife.

2 Rub fat into flour, using fingertips, until mixture looks like fine breadcrumbs. (Do not rub fat into flour for too long or the fat will begin to melt and your pastry will be difficult to handle).

3 Add exactly 2½ tablespoonfuls of cold water to flour mixture and mix in with a knife. Gently gather the mixture together (with your hand) to make a firm dough. The sides of the mixing bowl should be clean and the dough should not be sticky.

4 Leave pastry in a cool place until required. This recipe is the *basic recipe* for shortcrust pastry, and can be used to make many things, such as those on the following pages.

jam tarts

INGREDIENTS

Basic recipe for shortcrust pastry
½–¾ of a jar of raspberry jam
A little flour

EQUIPMENT

Rolling pin
2 × 12 bun tins
Pastry cutter
Teaspoon

1 Put oven on at Gas Mark 7 (electricity 425°F/220°C).

2 Make pastry.

3 Sprinkle a little flour onto a clean table top and onto your rolling pin.

4 Shape pastry round, using your hands.

5 Roll out pastry lightly, using short sharp strokes, moving it on the table top to make sure it is not sticking. Sprinkle on more flour if needed. Roll in one direction only, or pastry may become stretched.

6 Roll out pastry quite thinly.

7 Choose a pastry cutter slightly larger than the top of the bun tins.

8 Cut out circles, as close together as possible.

9 Pile trimmings and reroll. You will need 20–24 pastry circles.

10 Place pastry in bun tins, press down slightly.

11 Put a small teaspoonful of jam in the centre of each pastry case. Do not over-fill, or the jam will boil over.

12 Bake towards the top of the oven for 10 minutes, until the pastry is just brown.

13 Remove from bun tins while still hot, and LEAVE TO COOL.

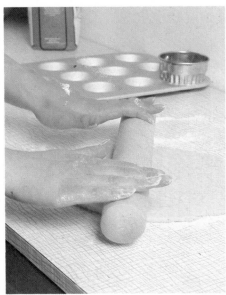

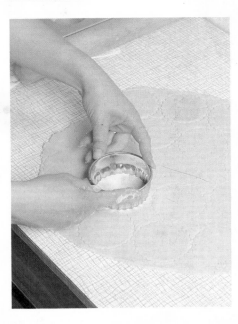

Variations

Follow method for jam tarts up to the end of stage 10, then prick base of each pastry case with a fork. Place in oven without filling and bake for 5–7 minutes until pastry is slightly brown. Remove from oven, put a teaspoonful of lemon curd in each pastry case and allow to cool.

Note

Lemon curd is not baked in the pastry as it is a rich mixture containing eggs and cooking may change both flavour and colour.

Mincemeat tart

INGREDIENTS

Basic recipe for shortcrust
pastry see page 42
3 tablespoonfuls mincemeat
A little flour

EQUIPMENT

Rolling pin
Table knife
25 cm (10 in) ovenproof plate

1 Put oven on at Gas Mark 7 (electricity 425°F/220°C).

2 Make pastry.

3 Sprinkle flour onto worktop and rolling pin and roll out pastry to fit the ovenproof plate.

4 Cover the plate with pastry and trim to fit.

5 Spread mincemeat over the 'well' part of the plate.

6 From the pastry left over, cut thin strips long enough to go right across the plate.

7 Using a little water to stick down the strips of pastry, make a criss-cross pattern over the top of the tart, twisting each strip once or twice.

8 Place in oven and bake for 10–15 minutes until pastry is slightly brown.

9 Allow to cool before eating.

Variations

If you don't like mincemeat you can make a tart of raspberry, pineapple or apricot jam. Use your strips of pastry to divide the tart into triangles of different coloured jams.

Note

If liked, pastry edge and strips can be brushed with water and sprinkled with sugar before baking.

Cheese straws

INGREDIENTS

100g (4 oz) flour
50g (2 oz) margarine
50g (2 oz) Cheddar cheese
Pinch of salt and pepper
1 egg

Optional:
1 teaspoonful dried parsley
1 pinch dry mustard

EQUIPMENT

Tablespoon
Table knife
Sieve
Mixing bowl
Rolling pin
Cheese grater
Baking tray
Fork

1. Put oven on at Gas Mark 6 (electricity 400°F/200°C).

2. Sift the flour and salt into the mixing bowl. Add the margarine and cut into small pieces. Rub together with your fingertips until the mixture looks like breadcrumbs.

3. Grate the cheese and stir it into the flour mixture, (add parsley).

4. Beat egg lightly with fork (add mustard).

5. Pour egg into mixture and mix with knife and then fingertips, to form a dough. (If the mixture is too dry add a few drops of cold water).

6. Roll out the dough on a floured surface and cut into long thin strips about 12 cm (5 in) long and 0.5 cm ($\frac{1}{4}$ in) wide.

7. Place on a lightly greased baking tray and put in the oven.

8. Bake for 10 to 15 minutes or until golden and firm at the edges.

9. Allow to cool. Cheese straws can be stored in an airtight tin.

Note

To make 'straw' bundles, cut circles with a pastry cutter and cut out the centre using a smaller cutter. When baked, place straws in rings.

Cheese & onion pasties

INGREDIENTS

Basic recipe for shortcrust pastry
(*page 42*)
100g (4 oz) Cheddar cheese
1 small onion
Salt and pepper
A little water
A little milk

EQUIPMENT

Rolling pin
Grater
Sharp knife
Plate
Pastry brush
Small basins
Baking sheet
Small plate or saucer
Mixing bowl

1 Put oven on at Gas Mark 6 (electricity 400°C/200°F).

2 Make pastry. Leave in a cool place.

3 Grate cheese onto plate, then put in mixing bowl.

4 Top, tail, peel and chop onion, (see page 13) add with a pinch of salt and pepper to cheese and mix well.

5 Sprinkle a little flour onto a clean table top and onto your rolling pin.

6 Shape pastry round, using your hands. Divide into four.

7 Roll out each piece lightly, using short sharp strokes and rolling in one direction only.

8 Roll out pastry quite thinly.

9 Using a saucer as a guide, cut one circle from each piece.

10 Pile trimmings together, re-roll, and cut out one more circle.

11 Divide cheese and onion mixture into five. Place on each pastry circle.

12 Brush edge of half of each pastry circle with water.

13 Fold one side over and press edges together. Place on baking sheet.

14 Pinch edges to decorate. Brush with milk to glaze.

15 Bake for 30 minutes or until pastry is golden brown.

Cornish pasties

INGREDIENTS

200g (8 oz) shortcrust pastry – see basic recipe on page 42
100g (4 oz) minced beef
1 tablespoonful grated onion
1 tablespoonful grated potato
Salt and pepper
Milk to glaze
A little water
A little flour

EQUIPMENT

As for Cheese and onion pasties

1 Put oven on at Gas Mark 6 (electricity 400°F/200°C).

2 Make pastry. Leave in a cool place.

3 Mix meat, onion, potato, and salt and pepper well together.

Follow recipe for *Cheese and onion pasties* from stage 5.

Sausage rolls

INGREDIENTS

Basic recipe for shortcrust pastry
(page 42)
or 1 small packet frozen puff pastry
8 skinless sausages
A little flour
A little milk
A little water

EQUIPMENT

Rolling pin
Pastry brush
Baking sheet
Small knife

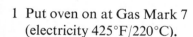

1 Put oven on at Gas Mark 7 (electricity 425°F/220°C).

2 Lightly sprinkle flour onto a clean table top and onto your rolling pin. If you have made your own pastry, shape it with your hands to an oblong.

3 Roll out the pastry to an oblong approximately 35 cm × 25 cm (14 in × 10 in).

4 Place sausages in 2 long rows down length of pastry (like a 'train' of sausages).

5 Brush inside edges of the pastry with a little water. Cut pastry down the centre of the two rows of sausages.

6 Roll pastry over sausages, sealing edges together and making sure that joins are underneath.

7 Divide each roll in two, then into four, and if wished into eight.

8 Place on a baking sheet. Brush with milk. Score the top of each sausage roll with a knife or snip with scissors.

9 Bake for 15–20 minutes until sausage rolls are a golden brown colour. Remove from baking sheet to cool.

 For easy cleaning leave baking sheet to soak in water before washing.

Party time

Cheese & pineapple hedgehog

INGREDIENTS

1 orange
200g (8 oz) Cheddar cheese
Medium can pineapple pieces
Cocktail sticks
1 cherry

EQUIPMENT

Small flat serving dish
Small sharp knife

1 Cut a small slice from one end of the orange to make it stand flat on the dish.

2 Cut cheese into 1 cm ($\frac{1}{2}$ inch) cubes.

3 Spear a piece of pineapple and a piece of cheese onto each cocktail stick. Push into orange.

Note

'Eyes' can be made using two halves of a cherry held in position with half a cocktail stick.
Pineapple may be changed for small seedless grapes or halved grapes, or a combination of the two fruits used.

Quiche

(pronounced keesh)

INGREDIENTS

*Basic recipe for shortcrust
pastry – see page 42*
Flour for rolling
2 rashers bacon
2 tomatoes
2 eggs
200–250 ml (½ pint) milk
50g (2 oz) Cheddar cheese
1 small onion
Salt and pepper

EQUIPMENT

Rolling pin
Measuring jug
Sharp knife
Fork
20 cm (8 in) ovenproof pie or flan dish
Chopping board

1 Put oven on at Gas Mark 5
   (electricity 375°F/190°C).

2 Make pastry, roll it out and line
   the flan dish.

3 Skin 1 tomato – spear on fork,
   hold over hotplate or gas flame
   until it 'pops'. Peel off skin.
   Thinly slice and lay over the base
   of the pastry.

4 Finely chop the small onion (see
   page 13) and sprinkle over the
   tomato.

5 Remove the rind from the bacon
   and cut rashers into tiny pieces.
   Add these to the dish.

6 Grate the cheese and sprinkle
   over the top of all the other
   ingredients.

7 Beat the eggs into the milk and
   add salt and pepper.

8 Pour this carefully over the cheese.

9 Bake for 30–40 minutes or until
   set. Allow to cool slightly before
   serving.

10 Decorate the top with the other
    tomato sliced thinly.

Mint chocolate birthday cake

INGREDIENTS

150g (6 oz) caster sugar
150g (6 oz) margarine
150g (6 oz) self-raising flour
3 eggs
½ teaspoonful green food colouring
½ teaspoonful peppermint essence
1 dessertspoonful cocoa
1 tablespoonful hot water

for the filling and decoration:
350g (14 oz) icing sugar
125g (5 oz) butter
2 dessertspoonfuls cocoa
1 tablespoonful hot water
150g (6 oz) chocolate sugar strands

EQUIPMENT

Mixing bowl
Sieve
Wooden spoon
Small basin
Small mixing bowl
2 × 18 cm (7 in) tins

1 Put oven on at Gas Mark 4 (electricity 350°F/180°C).

2 Make the mixture using the creaming method on page 30.

3 Put half this mixture in another mixing bowl and add the cocoa dissolved in the hot water.

4 To the other half of the mixture add the food colouring and the peppermint essence. Place in tins.

5 Bake both cakes for 20 minutes. When slightly cool turn out onto a wire rack, cover with a clean damp tea towel and leave to cool completely.

6 Using 250g (10 oz) icing sugar and the butter, make up the butter icing by creaming the ingredients together with half the cocoa.

7 Sandwich the two cakes together with the butter icing and spread icing round the sides, taking it just over the top edge. Dip the

sides in chocolate sugar strands and place on a serving plate.

8 With the remaining icing sugar make glacé icing (see page 31). Remove one tablespoonful of this and colour it green. Put the green icing in a paper icing bag and either fit a number 2 writing

nozzle or snip off the end of the bag. Flavour the rest of the glacé icing with cocoa.

9 Pour chocolate icing on the top of the cake and when set pipe 'Happy Birthday' with green icing. Arrange candles in the icing round the edge and serve.

Apricot baskets

INGREDIENTS

To make 10 – 12

½ the basic recipe for the all-in-one or creamed mixture (pages 28 or 30)

400g (1 lb) tin apricot halves

1 packet orange Quick-Jel

Angelica strips

Butter icing or fresh cream

EQUIPMENT

As for cake mixture

10 – 12 cake cases

Small pan

1 Follow the method for the basic mixture and divide between the paper cake cases.

2 Bake for 15 minutes (Gas Mark 5, electricity 375°F/190°C) and when cool, level off the tops if necessary.

3 Make up a glaze following the instructions on the packet of Quick-Jel.

4 Dip each apricot in the glaze and place one on top of each cake. Pipe cream round the edge of each cake.

5 Cut a thin strip of angelica to form each handle. Serve.

HAPPY BIRTHDAY

Easter cake *or simnel cake*

INGREDIENTS

500g (1 lb 4 oz) mixed dried fruit
200g (8 oz) plain flour
Pinch of salt
Level teaspoonful cinnamon
Level teaspoonful ground nutmeg
150g (6 oz) margarine
150g (6 oz) brown sugar
3 eggs
1 tablespoonful apricot jam
400g (1 lb) almond paste (see page 55)

EQUIPMENT

Mixing bowl
Wooden spoon
Rolling pin
18 cm (7 in) deep cake tin
Piece of wide ribbon
Sieve
Small basin
Fork

1 Grease and line a deep 18 cm (7 in) cake tin (see page 56).

2 Put oven on at Gas Mark 3 (electricity 325°F/160°C).

3 Divide the almond paste into three, making one piece slightly smaller than the other two.

4 Cream margarine and sugar well together and gradually add the eggs (as for creamed mixture page 30). Add the dried fruit, and finally sift in the flour and spice.

5 Roll out one third of the almond paste to roughly the shape of the tin. Place half of the cake mixture into the tin, put in the almond paste and cover with the remaining mixture.

6 Bake for 2–2½ hours until all sound of bubbling has stopped. (Because of the layer of almond paste, it is not possible to test with a skewer.) Leave to cool in the tin.

7 With the second large piece of almond paste, roll out to the shape of the cake top and while still in the tin, brush the cake top with apricot jam and press the almond paste in place.

8 Remove cake from tin.

9 Out of the smallest piece of almond paste, shape 11 eggs. Decorate top with a fork pressed down round the edge to make a pattern.
Brush the almond paste with jam and put eggs around edge.

10 Place under the grill until evenly brown.

11 Tie a ribbon round the cake and serve.

Easter nests

INGREDIENTS
100g (4 oz) chocolate
2 Shredded Wheat portions
100g (4 oz) coloured sweets

EQUIPMENT
Small basin
Pan
Wooden spoon
Small paper cake cases

1 Melt chocolate in small basin over pan of boiling water.

2 Break up Shredded Wheat, add chocolate and stir well.

3 Place in cake cases, press centre down to shape nest.

4 Leave to set in cool place.

5 Fill with sugar eggs or sweets. (You can make marzipan eggs and dip them in coffee, see photograph.)

Christmas cake

INGREDIENTS

700g (1¾ lb) mixed dried fruit
75g (3 oz) glacé cherries
50g (2 oz) almonds (flaked or chopped)
1 teaspoonful lemon rind – grated
200g (8 oz) plain flour
½ teaspoonful mixed spice
½ teaspoonful cinnamon
150g (6 oz) butter
150g (6 oz) brown sugar
3 eggs (size 2–3)

EQUIPMENT

Mixing bowl	Fork
Wooden spoon	Sieve
Small basin	Grater

Either 20 cm (8 in) round tin
Or 18 cm (7 in) square tin

Cooking time: 3 hours

1. Put oven on at Gas Mark 3 (electricity 325°F/160°C).

2. Grease and line the baking tin (see page 56).

3. Weigh all the ingredients.

4. Place butter in the bowl and soften with a wooden spoon. Add sugar and mix well together.

5. Gradually add beaten eggs. If mixture begins to curdle, place bowl in hot water or add 1 tablespoonful sieved flour and beat well.

6. Add the dried fruit, nuts, cherries and lemon rind and mix well in.

7. Sift flour with spices and add to mixture. Stir well so that all ingredients are very well mixed.

8. Put mixture in tin and slightly hollow out centre. This ensures a flat surface after cooking.

9. Bake at Gas Mark 3 (electricity 325°F/160°C) for first hour then reduce heat to Gas Mark 2 (electricity 300°F/150°C) until cooked. Test using a skewer.

10. Leave cake to cool in the tin. Then take cake out of tin and remove paper.

Note

Spirit (e.g. sherry or brandy) can be added to improve the cake's flavour. *ASK AN ADULT FIRST.* Make holes with a skewer and pour spirit in. Putting it in after cooking makes sure you get full flavour. If it is added during cooking much of it evaporates and the flavour is lost.

Almond paste

The first layer is almond paste which can be made or bought. Either buy the stated quantity or make up the following recipe.

Top only (300g (¾ lb) almond paste)

INGREDIENTS
150g (6 oz) ground almonds
75g (3 oz) caster sugar
75g (3 oz) icing sugar
Few drops almond essence
1–2 egg yolks
Icing sugar for rolling
Apricot jam

EQUIPMENT
Mixing bowl
Rolling pin
Cake board 23 cm (9 in) across
String

(Top and sides – you want an extra 200–300g (½–¾ lb) of almond paste)

1 Mix almonds and sugar together.

2 Mix egg yolks with almond essence.

3 Mix ingredients together. (You will find it easier to mix with your hand which will soften the oils in the almonds.)

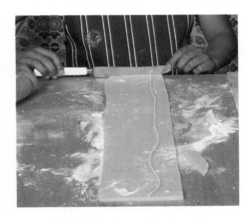

Covering a cake with almond paste

Top:

1 If top of cake is uneven, trim so that it will sit well on cake board. Either the top or the base of the cake can be used as a base for decoration.

2 Sprinkle the work surface with icing sugar. Roll out ⅓ of almond paste (if covering top and sides) making a circle or a square to fit your cake.

3 Brush the top of the cake with jam and turn it over onto the almond paste. Press down well and using a sharp knife, trim the edges.

Sides:

4 Measure around the cake with a piece of string and use this as a guide when rolling. Sprinkle work surface well with icing sugar and keeping almond paste as a long strip, roll to the same length as the string. Square off one end.

5 Brush cake sides well with apricot jam.

6 Place cake on almond paste and roll over, pressing down well.

7 Level off the other end and press the join together until smooth.

8 Smooth top join. Place on a cake board 23 cm (9 in) across.

9 If royal icing is to be applied within 2–3 days, brush all almond paste with egg white. (This stops the oils from the almonds discolouring the white icing.) OR you can leave lightly covered for a week to ten days to dry out naturally.

10 Store any left over pieces of almond paste in a polythene bag.

Royal icing

INGREDIENTS
Top only: 300g (¾ lb) icing sugar
Top and sides: 500g (1¼ lb) icing sugar

EQUIPMENT
Mixing bowl
Wooden spoon
Teaspoon
Palette knife or spatula

The consistency of royal icing is very important. If this is your first attempt at decorating a Christmas cake, a rough icing finish is easiest to achieve but there is no reason why piped icing cannot be used as well for a special effect.

1 To each 500g of sieved icing sugar use 2 egg whites, 1 teaspoonful lemon juice and 2 teaspoonfuls glycerine (which stops the icing drying too hard).

2 Place egg whites in mixing bowl, add lemon juice and glycerine. Gradually add sieved icing sugar and mix with a wooden spoon until the mixture is smooth and shiny and will stand up in soft peaks when lifted with the spoon.

3 Place icing in the centre of the top of the cake and with a palette knife or spatula, spread the icing over the top and down the sides to the board.

4 Using the knife, draw up the icing in soft peaks. If you are going to pipe some decorations, smooth out required area on top using a hot, dry knife.

5 Leave to set for 2–3 days.

Almond paste decorations

Using left over almond paste, colour with green or red food colouring and cut out holly leaves and berries.

Leave uncoloured for mistletoe. Use a tiny amount of royal icing to stick the decorations in place.

You can buy decorations for the top of your cake if you prefer.

Lining tins

1 For square tin, brush base and sides with oil. Then cut two squares of greaseproof paper, one to fit the base and one 2.5 cm (1 in) bigger all round. Lay base of tin on the larger square and cut a 2.5 cm (1 in) frill all round as shown.

2 Put the base back in the tin and line with the greaseproof paper. Make sure the frill lies flat against the sides.

3 Cut two strips to fit round the sides of the tin but 5 cm (2 in) taller than the sides and cut a 2.5 cm (1 in) frill along one edge as shown. Line the sides making the frill lie flat on the base and brush with oil.

4 Insert the second square of greaseproof paper to cover the base.

The method is the same for a round tin.

Orange & lemon fizz

INGREDIENTS
Makes 1 litre (2 pints)
1 lemon
250 ml (½ pint) orange squash
1 bottle lemonade
Ice cubes

EQUIPMENT
Lemon squeezer
Small sharp knife
Jug
Glasses

1 Cut lemon in half and cut one half into 3–4 slices. Squeeze juice from other half, place in jug.

2 Add orange squash and ice cubes. Pour on lemonade.

3 Float lemon slices on top and serve.

Still lemonade

INGREDIENTS
1 lemon
250 ml (½ pint) water
25g – 50g (1 oz – 2 oz) sugar to taste
Ice cubes

EQUIPMENT
Vegetable peeler
Strainer
Lemon squeezer

1 Thinly pare lemon rind using vegetable peeler. Place in small pan.

2 Squeeze juice from lemon, place in pan. Add 250 ml (½ pint) water, bring to boil. Boil for 1 minute. Leave to cool, add sugar to taste.

3 Strain into serving jug, top with ice cubes and serve.

Variations

Oranges or limes can also be used. Alter the amount of sugar added to suit your taste.

Banana milk shake

INGREDIENTS
1 banana
2 scoops of icecream
500 ml (1 pint) milk
1 rounded tablespoonful (25g or 1 oz) of sugar

EQUIPMENT
2 glasses
Fork
Mixing bowl
Whisk

1 Peel banana, put in bowl and mash with the fork.

2 Add sugar and milk, and whisk until frothy.

3 Pour into glasses, top with a scoop of icecream, and drink at once.

Variations

Milk shakes can be made using different flavoured milk shake syrups. All of these can then be topped with a scoop of icecream.

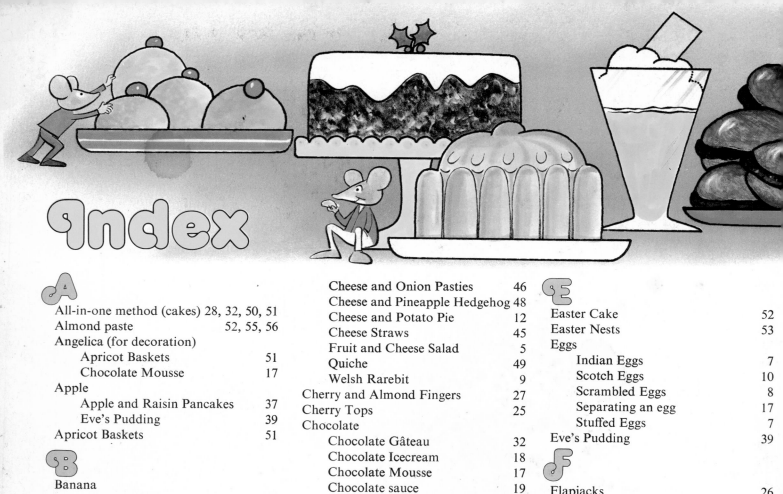

Index